W9-BLH-231

LIBRARY OF CONGRESS CATALOG NUMBER: 82-0500830

ISBN 0-934738-03-3

Photographs © 1982 in U.S.A. by Robert Llewellyn. Photographs © under UCC 1982 by Robert Llewellyn. All rights reserved.

This book, or portions thereof, may not be reproduced in any form without permission of the publishers, Lickle Publishing, Inc. Photography may not be reproduced in any form without permission of Robert Llewellyn.

Printed in Hong Kong.

Page 7. From "Jefferson at Monticello: The Private Life of Thomas Jefferson" by Rev. Hamilton Wilcox Pierson in JEFFERSON AT MONTICELLO, edited by James A. Bear, Jr. copyright 1967 by the University Press of Virginia, reprinted by permission of the publisher.

*Published in 1996 by Thomasson-Grant & Lickle
106 South Street
Charlottesville, Virginia, 22902
804/977-1780*

THOMASSON-GRANT & LICKLE
New York • Charlottesville

The Academical Village
Thomas Jefferson's University

PHOTOGRAPHY BY ROBERT LLEWELLYN

ESSAY BY DOUGLAS DAY

WITH APPENDIX

CONSIDER THE COMMON PLAN followed in this country, but not in others, of making one large and expensive building, as unfortunately erroneous. It is infinitely better to erect a small and separate lodge for each separate professorship, with only a hall below for his class, and two chambers above for himself; joining these lodges by barracks for a certain portion of the students, opening into a covered way to give a dry communication between all the schools. The whole of these arranged around an open square of grass and trees, would make it, what it should be in fact, an academical village, instead of a large and common den of noise, of filth and of fetid air. It would afford that quiet retirement so friendly to study, and lessen the dangers of fire, infection and tumult. Every professor would be the police officer of the students adjacent to his own lodge, which should include those of his own class of preference, and might be at the head of their table, if, as I suppose, it can be reconciled with the necessary economy to dine them in smaller and separate parties, rather than in a large and common mess. These separate buildings, too, might be erected successively and occasionally, as the number of professors and students should be increased, as the funds become competent.

MY NEXT INSTRUCTION was to get ten able-bodied hands to commence the work. I soon got them, and Mr. Jefferson started from Monticello to lay off the foundation and see the work commenced. An Irishman named Dinsmore and I went along with him. As we passed through Charlottesville, I went to old Davy Isaacs' store and got a ball of twine, and Dinsmore found some shingles and made some pegs, and we all went on to the old field together. Mr. Jefferson looked over the ground some time and then stuck down a peg. He stuck the very first peg in that building, and then directed me where to carry the line, and I stuck the second. He carried one end of the line, and I the other, in laying off the foundation of the University. He had a little rule in his pocket that he always carried with him, and with this he measured off the ground and laid off the entire foundation, and then set the men at work. I have that rule now, and here it is," said Captain Bacon, taking it from a drawer in his secretary that he unlocked, to show it to us. It was a small twelve-inch rule, so made as to be but three inches long when folded up. "Mr. Jefferson and I were once going along the bank of the canal," said he, "and in crawling through some bushes and vines, it fell out of his pocket and slid down the bank into the river. Some time after that, when the water had fallen, I went and found it and carried it to Mr. Jefferson. He told me I had had a great deal of trouble to get it, and as he had provided himself with another, I could keep it. I intend to keep it as long as I live; and when I die, that rule can be found locked up in that drawer."

"After the foundation was nearly completed, they had a great time laying the cornerstone. The old field was covered with carriages and people. There was an immense crowd there. Mr. Monroe laid the cornerstone. He was President at that time. He held the instruments and pronounced it square. He only made a few remarks, and Chapman Johnson and several others made speeches. Mr. Jefferson—poor old man!—I can see his white head just as he stood there and looked on. After this he rode there from Monticello every day while the University was building, unless the weather was very stormy. I don't think he ever missed a day unless the weather was *very* bad. Company never made any difference. When he could not go on account of the weather, he would send me, if there was anything he wanted to know. He looked after all the materials and would not allow any poor materials to go into the building if he could help it. He took as much pains in seeing that everything was done right as if it had been his own house."

Captain Edmund Bacon (overseer of Monticello, 1806 to 1822) as recorded by the Rev. Hamilton W. Pierson.

The Quiet Place

by Douglas Day

LATE ONE EVENING in May, a friend and I were walking through a light, glowing haze of rain —fog laced with a faint trace of bourbon, really— up the West Lawn of the University. We stopped next to the Colonnade Club, the University's oldest building, so that I could quietly brag to her, with an insouciance that we Virginians fancy is ours alone, that both my great-grandfather and I had lived in Number 33, the student's room next door: he in 1851, and I in 1954. (I have noticed that other people, especially non-Virginians, do not find this small evidence of dynasty nearly as impressive as I do; but never mind.)

Graduation had taken place earlier that day. The lower levels of the Lawn were still cluttered with folding chairs and empty champagne bottles. No one had yet removed from the porch of Cabell Hall the walnut lectern from which some speaker doubtless had conventionally exhorted the grad-uating class that its life had only begun, and that it was time to bid a sad farewell to the fair tran-quillity of Mr. Jefferson's Academical Village, and go forth bravely into the real world.

"Sure, real world," a rather forlorn graduate, still in black gown and hoping to find a last party on the Lawn before the evening ended, said to us. "What about our new Depression? Do you know how many of us still don't have jobs? Don't ask. Who wouldn't want to stay on here?"

Well, some of us have been graduated in fat times, some in lean. My great-grandfather, Douglas, had built up his medical practice in Warrenton just in time to give it up and ride off with Jeb Stuart's cavalry. Glorious times, maybe, but soon very lean indeed. So much so, in fact, that my grandfather could not afford the $250 tuition the University wanted from him, and had to work in a bank to support the family, so that his sister, Virginia (of course), one of Warrenton's most sought-after belles, could come down to Charlottesville for grand balls and elegant picnics. The post-bellum University was much less rowdy than the ante-bellum: the family didn't have to worry that Aunt Virginia would have to witness duels, horse-whippings of professors, or the fatal shooting by a student of the Chairman of the Faculty, as had happened in 1840. (The Academical Village was, once founded, always a Village; but it was not always so Academical.)

My friend in 1982, though, saw the Lawn and Ranges not only as they had been, but also as they were this night. She commiserated with the forlorn, unemployed graduate, then steered me toward the Rotunda, softly lit and gleaming in the mist. I, like Faulkner's Quentin Compson, was wrapping myself up in the Past; but she was seeing *Things* as they were tonight, and making me see them, too: a giant ash tree behind one pavilion, with a trunk six feet thick and a height of at least a hundred feet; and, especially, the buildings Jefferson had designed to be not only beautiful, but beautiful in such a way as to lead their inhabitants to think, to learn in a place of precise and subtle loveliness.

I have seen the Rotunda perhaps two thousand times over the years, but each time I confront it it

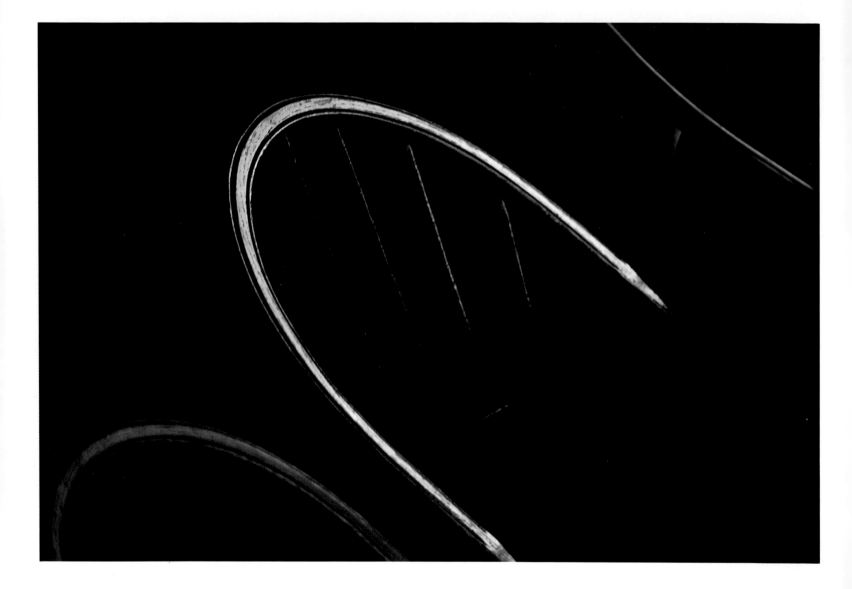

catches me by surprise: I am always seeing it for the first time. In fact, it's that way with *all* the old University: gardens, pavilions, Ranges, and the great Lawn. Jefferson designed it all so intricately, so cleverly, that what looks like perfect symmetry is actually perfect asymmetry: there is no one thing that quite matches with one other thing.

My friend did try, but I had got myself into the game of generations, and begun thinking of my own days, in the mid-Fifties. I had first come to the University for a prep-school track meet, and will always remember being vastly impressed by seeing a student sauntering about, dressed as I supposed all University men must dress: dark grey flannel suit, tattersall waistcoat, white bucks (dirty, it goes without saying), and walking stick. This splendid beau nodded casually to a friend as he passed, and remarked wanly about what a hangover he had. I knew from this moment that the ghost of my great-grandfather was going to have to move over and make room for me. This University was *mine.*

I *did* come to the University, the admissions policies being much less stringent then than now; and it was much as I had hoped it would be. I came in the Eisenhower years, and so never gave a thought to anything that went on outside Albemarle County. I joined one of the right fraternities (this was vital, clearly), bought the right kinds of clothes, played lacrosse (badly), got Gentlemen's C's, was never caught studying, and never let a professor know me well enough to connect my name with my face. I slipped up in the second semester of my last year, and accidentally made the Dean's List.

This small embarrassment proved useful, however, four years later, when, after a hitch in the Marines, I came back as a graduate student in English. (Students now are amazed to learn that in my time

at the University we all naturally assumed that we'd all go into one of the services — as officers, of course — before we took up our real careers.)

Nothing had changed in those four years: I saw the same intricate social hierarchy, the same clothes, the same sort of girls up from Sweet Briar or Hollins. But I was outside it all, now, married, twice a father, and compelled to get good grades. I came up onto the Lawn only on Sundays, to read the *New York Times* on the steps of the Rotunda while my sons climbed around on the statue of Homer and his ephebe. The rest of the time I spent like the few dreary grinds I had known during my undergraduate years: either in the stacks of Alderman Library or in the cinderblock-walled classrooms of New Cabell Hall. I remember nursing a secret resentment that someone else, probably not even a Virginian, was living in 33 West Lawn.

Then, in 1962, I joined the faculty; and *still* nothing seemed to have changed: the same polite and elusive students, all in tweed jackets and correct ties, hair neatly trimmed, no political opinions. One still saw signs around the edges of the Lawn, asking us not to walk on the grass.

Things began to happen around 1964, when the University leaders made a massive — and largely successful — move toward academic excellence. The Gentlemen's C turned into a B or better, it became almost respectable to study, women and Blacks joined us, the coat-and-tie tradition died almost overnight (even for the faculty, or at least for its younger members). We built ourselves an atomic reactor and started working with things like laser beams and electron microscopes. The student population doubled. The Library had to expand in order to contain immeasurably valuable new collections. The Academical Village now seemed more like a city — unless one took the trouble to walk up onto the

Lawn and look down toward the Rotunda. The benign silence was still there. I might be fighting for tenure, but I knew that this was still *my* University.

It was a different sort of place, though, when my oldest son came to it in the early Seventies. The war in Viet Nam was still interminably winding down, and finally even the old University grew sick of it. Our reaction was nothing compared with, say Berkeley's or Columbia's (and I don't mean to be prissy here, either: hell, we had a history not of locking deans in their offices, but of *shooting* them); but we handled it all pretty well, and got off with a few processions, sit-ins, and boycotts. For a few months, students and professors would shrilly and stridently argue about what texts were "relevant," ideologically or sexually speaking. It never occurred to my son, the youngest Douglas, to join a fraternity (nor would it have occurred to me to encourage him to do so.) He invented his own major, kept to himself, wore his hair shoulder-length, and did not attend his own graduation. I do not know whether he even *saw* any of Jefferson's buildings, let alone enter any of them. His grades were far better than mine had been. But I do not know that he learned very much: he, like many of the Viet Nam generation, looked at learning with scorn.

This influx of angry vigor subsided rapidly with the war's end, and many of us who are still at the University are a little sad about the return to the *status quo ante.* Today's students continue to work hard — not necessarily, though, because of the social and ethical relevance of an education. In our present lean years, they will not get a job, or be accepted in any sort of postgraduate program, unless they can present a transcript with a lot of gentlemen's — or ladies — A's on it. No student in the past four years has asked me to explain why I had chosen to teach a certain text, or why I had avoided another. I wish someone would.

My daughter is now a second-year woman at the University. She wears just the right sort of clothes, has joined one of the top sororities, plays lacrosse (well), and hopes that in her last year she will be allowed to live in 33 West Lawn. I hope she will be, and I'm sure my great-grandfather does, too, from his grave in Warrenton.

The University *is* a city, now, with new buildings spreading ever deeper into Charlottesville and even out into the County. But the Lawn and the Ranges are still there; the Academical Village is still intact, as beautiful and tranquil as ever: a constant and quiet center of our intellectual lives, even if we go for days buried in our drably modern offices and classrooms, almost never taking the time really to look at the most nearly-perfect academic structure yet designed.

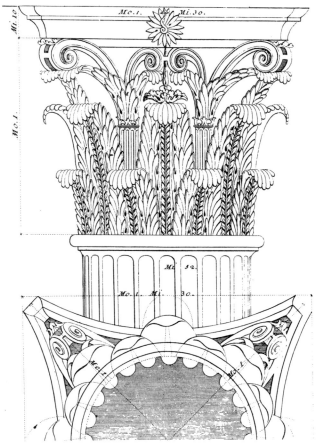

Book I, Plate XXVI; Palladio

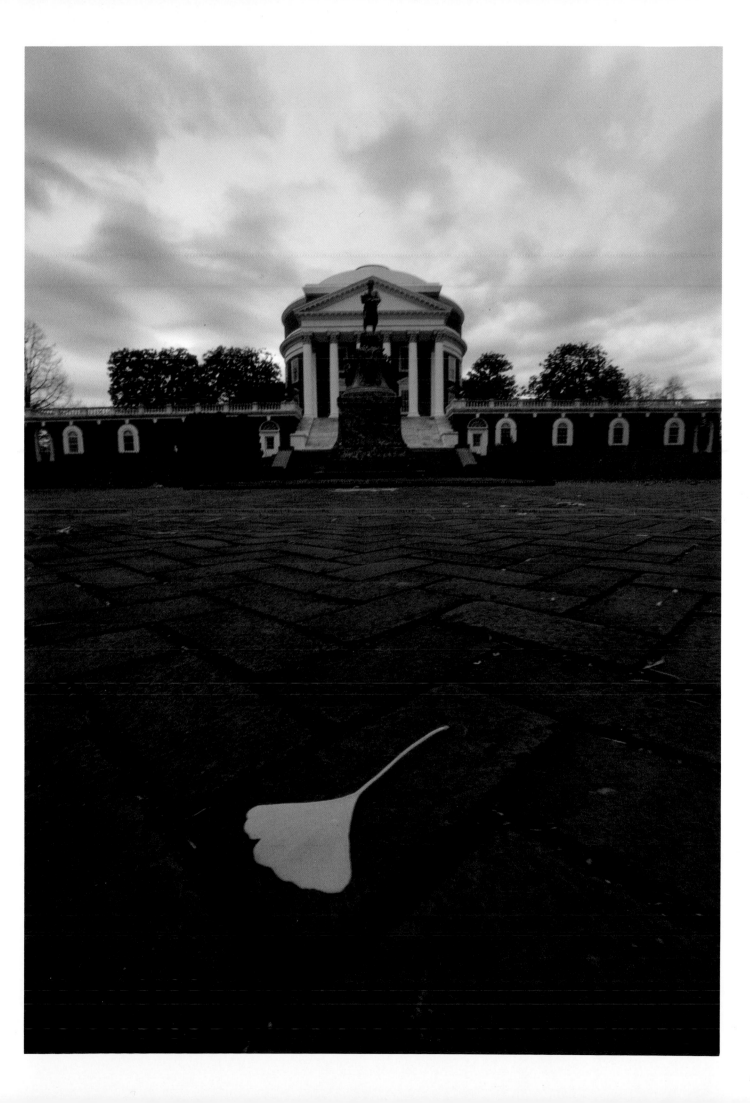

THIS INSTITUTION OF MY NATIVE STATE,
THE HOBBY OF MY OLD AGE,
WILL BE BASED ON
THE ILLIMITABLE FREEDOM
OF THE HUMAN MIND
TO EXPLORE
AND TO EXPOSE EVERY SUBJECT
SUSCEPTIBLE OF ITS CONTEMPLATION.

*I LOOK TO THE DIFFUSION OF LIGHT
AND EDUCATION
AS THE RESOURCE MOST TO BE RELIED ON
FOR AMELIORATING THE CONDITION,
PROMOTING THE VIRTUE,
AND ADVANCING THE HAPPINESS OF MAN.*

... THE ART OF REASONING BECOMES OF FIRST IMPORTANCE.
IN THIS LINE ANTIQUITY HAS LEFT US THE FINEST MODELS FOR
IMITATION; AND HE WHO STUDIES AND IMITATES THEM MOST
NEARLY, WILL NEAREST APPROACH THE PERFECTION OF THE ART.

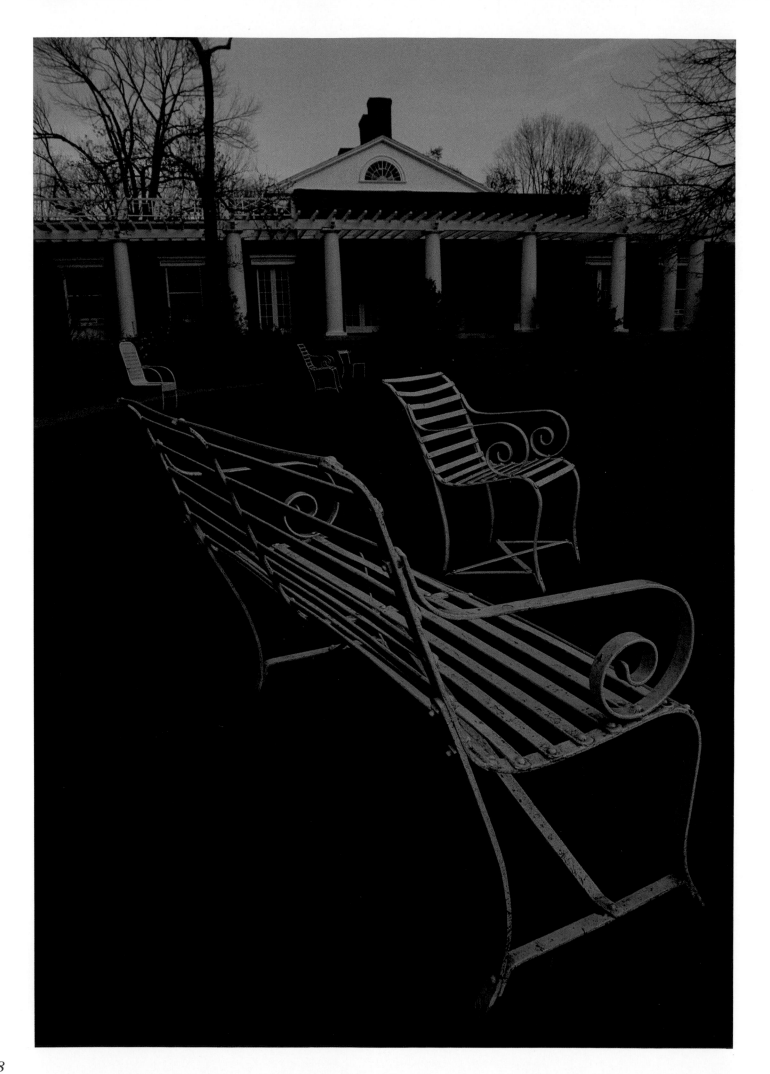

HERE, WE ARE NOT AFRAID TO FOLLOW TRUTH WHEREVER
IT MAY LEAD, NOR TO TOLERATE ANY ERROR SO LONG AS
REASON IS LEFT FREE TO COMBAT IT.

. . . I AM MYSELF AN EMPYRIC IN NATURAL PHILOSOPHY, SUFFERING MY FAITH TO GO NO FURTHER THAN MY FACTS. I AM PLEASED, HOWEVER, TO SEE THE EFFORTS OF HYPOTHETICAL SPECULATION, BECAUSE BY THE COLLISIONS OF DIFFERENT HYPOTHESES, TRUTH MAY BE ELICITED, AND SCIENCE ADVANCED IN THE END.

THE MARCH OF EVENTS
HAS NOT BEEN SUCH AS TO RENDER ITS COMPLETION
PRACTICABLE WITHIN THE LIMITS
OF TIME ALLOTTED TO ME;
AND I LEAVE ITS ACCOMPLISHMENT
AS THE WORK OF ANOTHER GENERATION…
THE ABOLITION OF THE EVIL IS NOT IMPOSSIBLE;
IT OUGHT NEVER THEREFORE TO BE DESPAIRED OF:
EVERY PLAN SHOULD BE ADOPTED,
EVERY EXPERIMENT TRIED,
WHICH MAY DO SOMETHING
TOWARDS THE ULTIMATE OBJECT.

…MINE, AFTER ALL, MAY BE A UTOPIAN DREAM, BUT BEING INNOCENT, I HAVE THOUGHT I MIGHT INDULGE IN IT TILL I GO TO THE LAND OF DREAMS, AND SLEEP THERE WITH THE DREAMERS OF ALL PAST AND FUTURE TIMES.

THOMAS JEFFERSON'S QUOTATIONS

PHOTOGRAPHS

1

POE'S ROOM, 13 WEST RANGE. Edgar Allan Poe came to the University of Virginia in February 1826. His stay was brief—he withdrew the following December. The Poe Room is maintained by the Raven Society, named at its founding in 1904 to honor the University's melancholy, best-known poet.

2

BRONZE FIGURE, JEFFERSON STATUE. Presented as a gift to the University by the sculptor, Sir Moses Ezekiel, the statue faces University Avenue on the north side of the Rotunda. A configuration of the Liberty Bell with four winged, female figures—Liberty, Justice, Religious Freedom, and Human Freedom—forms the base upon which stands the figure of Thomas Jefferson.

5

"THE CABINET." Jefferson completed many of the architectural drawings for the Academical Village in "The Cabinet," his study at Monticello. He referred frequently to his beloved Andrea Palladio's renderings of classical architecture, although his own copies had been sold to Congress with the bulk of his personal library. In all likelihood he completed many of his sketches working from a copy of Palladio's works he borrowed from James Madison.

6

PORTICO, THE ROTUNDA. Thomas Jefferson initially hoped to use native stone for the capitals of the columns in the Lawn area. But the local stone was not fine enough for carving, particularly for the delicate ecanthus leaves of the Corinthian capitals, so marble capitals were carved in Italy and imported.

8-9

AERIAL VIEW FROM EAST, THE ACADEMICAL VILLAGE. Visitors often assume that the large building on Lewis Mountain, the hill west of the University, is part of the Academical Village. It is in fact a private residence originally built by Gen. John Watts Kearney around 1909.

10

PLASTER WALL, WEST WING OF THE ROTUNDA.

12

WINDSOR CHAIRS, HOTEL C, JEFFERSON HALL, WEST RANGE. Jefferson Hall is home of the Jefferson Debating Society, established in 1825, the first year classes were held at the University. Oratorical societies were very popular at the Academical Village in the 19th century, although debates sometimes grew so heated that proceedings culminated in challenges to duel.

15

GINGKO LEAF, ROTUNDA WALK. The gingko, probably the oldest living species of tree, has changed little in the last 10 million years. Popular in Europe, the trees were introduced to the Grounds of the University by William Abbott Pratt, first superintendent of buildings and grounds, who planted the male gingko standing immediately northwest of the Rotunda around 1859. He received considerable criticism from faculty and students for replacing the large locusts and oaks already on the Grounds with such "fashionable" species.

16

CORINTHIAN CAPITAL, FROM PALLADIO.

17

NORTH VIEW OF ROTUNDA. In 1853 Robert Mills, who had studied drafting and architecture with Thomas Jefferson at Monticello, was commissioned to design a north Annex to the Rotunda for additional classroom space. The Annex extended a good distance toward University Avenue, but was completely destroyed by the fire that gutted the Rotunda in 1895.

18-19

AERIAL VIEW, THE ROTUNDA AND "THE CORNER." Madison Hall, fraternities and sororities on Madison Lane, shops, restaurants, banks, St. Paul's Episcopal Church, and apartment houses pack "The Corner," an outgrowth of the original Academical Village.

20

WEST LAWN.

21

PAVILION I, WEST LAWN.

23

LIBRARY SHELVES, DOME ROOM, THE ROTUNDA. In Thomas Jefferson's original design, the Rotunda was to serve as the University's library. Venetian blinds, which Jefferson regarded as both attractive and functional, are used in the windows of the Dome Room.

24-25

WEST RANGE. As at Monticello, Jefferson specified that brick for the University's buildings be made from earth near the building site. The brick columns of the West and East Range are called "Arcades" because of the arches between columns. There are three "Hotels," which originally served as student dining halls, on each Range.

26

PORTICO OF THE ROTUNDA. "If a nation expects to be ignorant and free, in a state of civilization," Thomas Jefferson wrote Col. Charles Yancey in 1816, "it expects what never was and never will be."

27

ROTUNDA CLOCK. The face of the clock is made of heavy boilerplate, since a favorite pastime of University students—even up through World War II—was to take target practice with rifles on the hands of the clock. Until the thin metal was replaced with iron plate, the target shooting played havoc with the clockworks. Firearms were prohibited from University property after WWII, a regulation Jefferson requested in 1825.

28

ENTRY, PAVILION IX. The recessed arch of the entryway to Pavilion IX extends to the second floor of the building, and light diffuses through the open area above the Colonnade roof.

29

ENTRY, UNIVERSITY CHAPEL. Distinctly not a part of Thomas Jefferson's design for the Academical Village, since his arguments for the separation of education and religion earned him the title "infidel" among the more zealous clergy of his time, the Chapel is now a part of University tradition.

30-31

COLONNADE, WEST LAWN. When poet James Hay, Jr., a member of the class of 1903, asked readers of his poem "The Honor Men" to remember "the purple shadows of the Lawn, the majesty of the Colonnades, and the dream of your youth," he may have had in mind a snowbound evening on the Lawn.

32

WEST COLONNADE.

33

NORTH STEPS, THE ROTUNDA. In 1824, the Rotunda was the site of a special dinner for the Marquis de Lafayette, French hero of the American Revolution, and a close friend of Thomas Jefferson. Thirteen toasts were offered for the original 13 states, with scores of toasts ensuing. The affair is said to have lasted three hours.

34-35

VIEW FROM SOUTH PORTICO, THE ROTUNDA. Cabell Hall stands at the end of the Lawn. Jefferson had envisioned the Lawn as open-ended, with a view of the mountains, and so it remained until 1899, when Cabell Hall was built. The open Lawn proved an irresistible lure to wandering livestock, however, and in 1828 a post and rail fence was built at the south end of the Lawn to prevent the "depredations of cattle and hogs." The problem persisted, forcing the faculty to assess a fine of $10 for each hog permitted by its owner to "linger" on the Grounds more than 24 hours.

36-37

DOME ROOM, THE ROTUNDA. The dome of the Rotunda is 77 feet in diameter, one-half the size of the dome of the Pantheon, the Roman temple which served as Jefferson's model. The skylight, or oculus, of the room, unlike that of the Pantheon, is glassed in for protection against the elements. Stanford White radically changed the interior of the Rotunda when he directed its reconstruction following the 1895 fire. A painstaking, three-year project completed in 1976 restored the Rotunda to Jefferson's design.

38

THE UNIVERSITY SINGERS.

39

CHARLOTTESVILLE UNIVERSITY AND COMMUNITY SYMPHONY ORCHESTRA. Music, which Thomas Jefferson described as "the favorite passion" of his soul, flourishes at the University of Virginia.

40-41

AERIAL VIEW, THE LAWN AND RANGES. Jefferson designed some of the Pavilion roofs to be flat, in the manner of classical temples. However, the Board of Visitors argued strongly that such roofing would cause leakage problems, and Jefferson agreed to install gabled roofs.

42

ROTUNDA, SOUTH PORTICO. Visible beyond the Rotunda columns is an Ionic column of Pavilion II, East Lawn.

43

THE ROTUNDA. In Jefferson's early sketches for the Academical Village, the north end of the Lawn was left vacant, designated only for some "principal building." When Jefferson had completed the drawings for the Rotunda, he was advised by friends in the Virginia legislature to proceed slowly in his plans to construct the building, since not a few of the legislators viewed his design for a university in the wilderness as "extravagant."

44-45

GARDEN BEHIND HOTEL C, JEFFERSON HALL.

46

LAWN AREA FROM ROOF OF UNIVERSITY HOSPITAL. The view shows the back of Pavilion VIII, which houses the President's administrative offices, and beyond, the facade of Pavilion VII, called the Colonnade Club, which serves as a faculty club. Pavilion VII was the first building constructed at the University.

47

LIBRARY, CLARK HALL. Clark Hall, once the University's School of Law, now houses the Department of Environmental Sciences and the Science and Technology Library.

48

FAN WINDOW, PAVILION VI.

49

PAVILION VI, EAST LAWN.

50-51
AERIAL VIEW, THE ACADEMICAL VILLAGE. An afternoon in early spring provides an ideal setting for a party in the garden behind Hotel A, home of *The Virginia Quarterly Review.*

52
VIEW FROM PAVILION I ATTIC, WEST LAWN.

53
CARR'S HILL. The President's home was designed by Stanford White for Edwin Alderman, the University's first president.

54-55
WEST LAWN.

56
PAVILION III, WEST LAWN.

57
APPLE TREES, WEST RANGE. A stained glass window of the University Chapel appears among the flowering crab apple trees in the garden behind Hotel A.

58
COLONNADE CLUB GARDEN, PAVILION VII.

59
AERIAL VIEW, THE ROTUNDA. While the buildings themselves were modeled upon the finest achievements of classical architecture, the concept of integrating buildings into an academical community was unique to Thomas Jefferson. One of the great achievements of American architecture, the Academical Village is all the more re-markable in that Jefferson was 73 years old when he undertook the first drawings.

60
PAVILION III GARDEN, WEST LAWN.

61
GARDEN GATE, PAVILION II, EAST LAWN.

62
PAVILION I GARDEN. The Serpentine Walls, which are only one brick thick, were designed by Thomas Jefferson for their strength, economy, and beauty. By the 20th century, the walls and gardens had suffered significant damage and alteration. Through the gen-erosity and hard work of The Garden Club of Virginia, the Serpen-tine Walls were completely restored and the gardens replanted.

63
AERIAL VIEW, PAVILION VII GARDEN.

64-65
VIEW FROM LEWIS MOUNTAIN. Over a century of architectural styles is seen in this view from Lewis Mountain. Left to right are Memorial Gymnasium, Alderman Library, the Rotunda, and beyond the sycamores, Brooks Museum.

66-67
CABELL HALL. Designed by Stanford White, the building is named for Joseph C. Cabell, Thomas Jefferson's close friend in the Virginia legislature who played a vitally important role in securing legislative approval for the creation of the University of Virginia.

68-69
EIGHT-MAN SHELL, RIVANNA RESERVOIR. The Rives Boat Club, the first organized rowing team at the University, began prac-tice on the Rivanna River in 1877.

70
CLASSROOM, THORNTON HALL. According to an advertise-ment announcing the University of Virginia's first academic session, a candidate "for admission into the school of Mathematics, Natural Philosophy, or Natural History must be well acquainted with the elementary operations of Numerical Arithmetic, with Fractions, Vulgar and Decimal, and the extraction of the Roots—and to enter any school he must be 16 years of age, vigorously proved."

71
KRYPTON ION LASER. Research using laser spectroscopy to analyze the structure of atoms and molecules is conducted by the University's Physics Department. Lasers are located in the Accel-erator Building on Observatory Mountain.

72-73
PROCESSIONAL MANTLE, BOARD OF VISITORS. Trustees of the University of Virginia are called Visitors, and wear a mantle of blue and orange—the University's colors—in academic processions. Following the Civil War, the school colors were gray and red, sym-bolizing a Confederate uniform stained with blood. In 1888, a group of athletes, complaining of the lack of visibility of those colors in muddy field sports, adopted the colors blue and orange.

74
ACADEMIC PROCESSION, THE LAWN.

75
MACE OF THE UNIVERSITY OF VIRGINIA. Carried by the University Marshal in academic processions, the mace was presented as a gift to the University by the Seven Society, a secret organization active in University life. The sterling silver globe bears engravings of various University scenes, Jefferson's monogram, and the seal of the University.

76-77
FAN MOUNTAIN OBSERVATORY. The Fan Mountain facilities, 16 miles south of the central Grounds of the University, feature a 40-inch astrometric reflector telescope and a 32-inch Cassegrain reflector telescope. The telescopes are positioned at an altitude of 1,819 feet.

78
JEFFERSON STATUE, WEST LAWN. Karl Bitter completed the seated figure of Thomas Jefferson in 1915. Its marble base bears Jefferson's words on his founding of the Academical Village: "I am closing the last scene of my life by fashioning and fostering an estab-lishment for the instruction of those who come after us. I hope that its influence on their virtue, freedom, fame, and happiness will be salutary and permanent." The dream of Thomas Jefferson still lives.

The publisher gratefully acknowledges the support of:

James W. Bradshaw, President, The Bradshaw Group
Hilton Head Island, South Carolina

John B. Rogan, President, The Boar's Head Inn
Charlottesville, Virginia

John W. Williams, President, Anderson Brothers Bookstore
Charlottesville, Virginia